J   62-7075
351.003
Johnson, Gerald W.
PRESIDENCY, THE

THE
PRESIDENCY

Illustrated by Leonard Everett Fisher

New York

WILLIAM MORROW AND COMPANY

1962

THE
PRESIDENCY

BY
GERALD W. JOHNSON

TO

CHRISTOPHER VAN DEN HONERT,
American citizen-in-the-making.

Contents

Illustrations

THE PRESIDENCY

What the
President Does

In the city of Washington the 1600 block of Pennsylvania Avenue has only one house. It is the residence of the President of the United States.

From outside it looks rather plain, and compared to the residences of the heads of some other great nations it is small. Buckingham Palace, where the queen of England lives, and Schönbrunn Palace, where the emperor of Austria-Hungary used to live, are both larger, while the Palace of Versailles, where the king of France once lived, is many times larger.

Yet this residence that the people call the White House, although its official name is the Executive Mansion, is a palace in the true sense. It has 132 rooms. Merely to rebuild the interior a few years ago—it had stood so long that it had become unsafe—cost nearly six million dollars. It houses not one family only, but a great many other people— assistants to the President, secretaries, clerks, stenographers, typists, messengers, guards, and domestic servants. In 1960, 358 people were employed there full time, and 47 others part time.

Plainly, this is no ordinary city house, but what makes it a palace is that it is the residence of a ruler. We often use the word loosely, calling any fine, large building a palace, but that is not exact. Strictly speaking, a palace is the house of a man who has lawful power over a great many other people. Usually, but not always, he is a king, or emperor, or some other head of a political state. Sometimes he is a religious authority. We say that the bishop of London lives in Lambeth Palace, and the bishop of Rome, who is the pope, lives in the palace of the Vatican.

The man who lives in the White House is like a king in that his power is political, but he differs from both kings and bishops because he holds lawful power for only a limited time—four years. If his authority is renewed at the end of the fourth year, he may hold it for four more, but under no circumstances can he hold it for longer than ten

years. The ten-year limit makes it possible for a
Vice-President filling out an unexpired term to
have two full terms of his own. However, nearly
a third of our Presidents have been refused a second term.

Throughout his term the President is the head
of a very great nation, and is as much a ruler as
any king or emperor. This makes it correct to call
his residence a palace, although Americans seldom
do so, because when they think of palaces they
think of kings, and we did away with kings and
everything connected with them long ago.

As a matter of fact, the President today has more
power than most of the few remaining kings. This
is not as startling as it sounds, because it is only
in fairy tales that a king has all power and can
cut off the head of anyone who displeases him. In
the real world no man can rule a nation by himself. He has to have the help of a great many others,
and to get it he must pay some attention to what
they think. Even in the old days a king did not remain a king very long if everybody—soldiers, po-
licemen, judges, churchmen, merchants, and all the
rest—turned against him. A king is today, and for
a very long time has been, merely the head of the

state, whose duty is to enforce the laws and protect honest people against robbers, other criminals, and foreign enemies.

That is exactly what the President of the United States is supposed to do. The difference between him and such a ruler as Elizabeth II, Queen of England, is, first, that the President does a great deal more actual ruling than the Queen, who leaves everything to the prime minister and the cabinet. Second, at the end of four years the President must either be re-elected or hand over his power to a new President.

If you think that over carefully, you will find in it the idea that made our government different from every other government that existed when the United States of America first became a nation. On a certain day in a certain year the head of this nation must give up his power unless it has been renewed for four more years. He must. Whether he likes it or not makes no difference; he is obliged to get out.

As a matter of fact, being President is so hard a job that by the time he has held it for eight years a man is usually glad, rather than sorry, to give it up. But that isn't the point. The point is

that in this country there is a power that can say to the head of the state, "Go!" and he has to go. This power is the will of the people, and our Constitution says that it is right for the people to hold and use this power.

Of course, if the President actually commits a crime we can get rid of him at any time. The House of Representatives can pass what is called a bill of impeachment, reciting what he is accused of doing, and present it to the Senate. The Senate then considers it, and if two thirds of the Senators agree that he really has committed a crime, they can pass the bill, and immediately the Vice-President becomes President. But first the Senate must hear what the President and his lawyers have to say in his defense, and, to make sure that the hearing is fair, the Chief Justice must preside. This process has been tried only once, against President Andrew Johnson, and then it failed; it is extremely unlikely that it will be tried again.

In the beginning, and for a good many years after the beginning, the people in Europe, who were supposed to know most about how nations manage their affairs, said that the American system would never work. But it has worked. Yet if

you know the tremendous number of things t
must be looked after in the little palace on Penns
vania Avenue, you may be astonished that it l
worked at all.

George Washington was President of the Unite
States. John Fitzgerald Kennedy is President
the United States. The difference between thes
statements, as they appear in print, seems to be n
more than the change of *was* to *is*. So they seen
to declare that two men held the same job at dif
ferent times, but that is an error.

The job is not now what it was then in much
of anything except its title. The reason is that
Washington became President in 1789, Kennedy
in 1961, and in the 172 years between them the
whole world has changed, and the job of being
President has changed along with everything else.

If Washington could walk into Kennedy's office
today, he would have no idea what to do with a
typewriter, or a telephone, or a dictating machine,
or a light switch, or a match, or a sheet of carbon
paper, or a ball-point pen, for none of these things
existed when he was alive.

On the other hand, it is probable that someone
would have to show President Kennedy how to

mind. They know, as we all know, that Washington was a very wise man. So when a President in our time does something that Washington would never have done, these people promptly say that the modern man is a foolish fellow who ought not to be President. That could be true, but it does not have to be true. There are many things that Washington never thought of that a twentieth-century President must do.

If you wish to understand what President Kennedy actually does, you will not get much help from reading the Constitution. It mentions only five duties that he shall discharge. In the order in which they are named in Article Two of the Constitution they are: (1) the President shall command the armed forces, (2) he shall have power to require reports in writing from the heads of departments, (3) he shall make treaties with foreign nations, (4) he shall appoint officials of the United States, and (5) he shall enforce the laws and recommend to Congress new laws that may be needed.

These duties cover a great deal of ground — pretty nearly enough to make the President boss of the whole country, if he could do as he pleased about them. But he cannot. In discharging his five duties he is hedged about with close restrictions. He is, indeed, commander in chief of the armed forces; he can say that this general shall command that post, and this regiment shall go here, and that fleet shall go yonder, and he is obeyed. But he cannot say how large any of the armed forces shall be, and he cannot declare war on another nation. These rights belong to Congress. He can compel the members of his Cabinet to explain in writing exactly what they are doing, and why, and he can discharge them when he sees fit. But in appointing officers and in making treaties he must have the consent of the Senate, and the only laws he can enforce are those made by Congress. He can recommend new laws, but he cannot enact them. Only Congress can do that.

On the other hand, no bill passed by Congress becomes a law until the President has signed it, except in two cases. If he dislikes a bill, he can refuse to sign it and return it to Congress with a message explaining why he refused to sign. This is known as a veto, from a Latin word meaning *to forbid*. Then Congress can consider it again, and if at least two thirds of the Representatives and two thirds of the Senators vote for it a second time, it becomes law without the President's signature. That is the first exception. If the President allows ten days to pass after he receives a bill without either signing or sending it back, it becomes law. That is the second exception.

Someone pointed out that this left the way open for Congress to work a trick. It might pass a whole mass of bills that the President considered dreadful, and then adjourn the same day, before he had time to send them back. So to prevent this trick it is provided that if Congress adjourns before the ten days are up, then an unsigned bill does not become law. The popular saying is that if the President does not choose to sign the bill within those ten days, he just puts it in his pocket, so that kind of veto is called a pocket veto.

The five things that the Constitution says the President shall do seem quite simple, but even in Washington's time they were not as simple as they looked. The work of the government was already far more than one man could possibly supervise, so it had been separated into departments. Of the five duties there was only one that the Constitution makers expected the President to attend to personally—that was to inform Congress of what was going on and to recommend any changes in the law that he thought were needed. The other four he might turn over to department heads, although he must see that they do their work properly.

In his own office he got along with a secretary and two or three clerks, besides domestic servants. But as the country grew, more and more people were required until, by the time of Mr. Eisenhower's administration, the President's staff had fifty-one people, and more than four hundred people worked in or around the White House.

And that is only the start of it. In Washington's time the whole government employed only two or three thousand people other than soldiers and sailors in the Army and Navy. In Kennedy's time it is employing more than two million civilians, with three million in uniform in the armed services. Of the two million only a few thousands are employed by the legislative and the judiciary branches of the government; that is, by Congress and the courts. All the rest belong to the executive branch, and their work is directed by the President.

A great many, of course, are minor employees,

not requiring his attention. But the important officers, who have to be chosen by the President, now
number several thousands. One man cannot possibly keep track of all of them, so when it is necessary for the President to appoint an officer in some
distant state or to a job about which he doesn't
know much, he usually takes the advice of someone who knows both the man and what he is supposed to do. This adviser may be a Cabinet officer,
or a bureau chief, or a member of Congress from
the state concerned, or anyone else in whose judgment the President has confidence.

As a rule this system works pretty well, but
there is one catch in it. If the President takes the
wrong advice, he will appoint the wrong man, and
there will be trouble; then the people who have
to deal with this man will blame the President.
Sometimes the adviser, especially when he is a
member of Congress anxious to be re-elected, is
more interested in getting a good job for one of
his friends than in getting a good man for the job.
That happened so often at first that in 1883 a law
was passed setting up the Civil Service Commission, a board whose duty it is to hold examinations
to find people qualified for the smaller government

jobs. The person who gets the highest mark—or perhaps one of the three highest marks—gets the job, and the President doesn't have to bother with it. If the man turns out to be no good the Commission is blamed, not the President.

Even so, the amount of work done in the President's office is enormous. It is the headquarters of a nation of a hundred and eighty million people, and the amount of business—important business, not mere foolishness—that comes to it can hardly be imagined.

The President has two different kinds of secretaries. One kind, such as the Appointments Secretary, who arranges the time at which the President will see visitors, is actually a servant of the President. The other kind, such as the Secretary of the Treasury, the man in charge of all the government's money, is a member of the Cabinet and one of the great officers of state, responsible to Congress as well as to the President.

What is called the President's Cabinet is something that was not planned by the Constitution makers. It simply grew up because it was needed. There is not a word about it in the Constitution, and no law says that there shall be a Cabinet. It

came out of the plain, common-sense knowledge that no one man could look after all the work of the government, so it must be split into departments, each under a principal officer responsible to the President.

The departments had already been set up under the Articles of Confederation, and the Constitution, written later, simply gave the President authority over all of them. There were four when Washington became President: one to deal with foreign nations (State Department), one to deal with money matters (Treasury Department), one to handle the Army and Navy (War Department), and one to deal with legal questions (Department of Justice). The principal officers were the Secretary of State, the Secretary of the Treasury, the Secretary of War, and the Attorney General.

To head these departments Washington chose the best men he could get. Two of them, Thomas Jefferson, Secretary of State, and Alexander Hamilton, Secretary of the Treasury, are to this day regarded as among the greatest American statesmen. Washington knew that the advice of such men was highly valuable, so he consulted them on every important matter that came up. Every President since has consulted experts, and that is how the Cabinet came to exist.

However, as time passed and the country and its business grew, four departments were not enough, so others were established, one by one. First, the business of the post office became too much for the Secretary of the Treasury to handle along with his other duties; so it was set up as a separate department, and the Postmaster General became a member of the Cabinet. Others were added from time to time, until now there are ten.

The principal officers of these departments, eight Secretaries, the Attorney General, and the Postmaster General, are, after the President himself, the most important people in the executive branch of the government. The head of the Cabinet is the Secretary of State, who may be described as the fifth highest ranking officer in the whole government. If anything should happen to the President, Vice-President, Speaker of the House, and President pro tempore of the Senate (its regular presiding officer is the Vice-President), the Secretary of State would automatically become President.

After the Secretary of State come:

The Secretary of the Treasury, who handles the money;

The Secretary of Defense, in charge, under the President, of the armed forces;

The Attorney General, whose business is enforcing the law;

The Postmaster General, head of all the post offices in the country;

The Secretary of the Interior, in charge of all government property, except military property;

The Secretary of Agriculture, who looks after farmers and farming;

The Secretary of Commerce, who looks after businessmen and business;

The Secretary of Labor, who looks after wage earners other than farm hands;

The Secretary of Health, Education, and Welfare, who looks after those matters.

All these officers are appointed by the President, and each is required by law to advise him on any matter that comes under his department. But really big questions almost never concern one department alone. War, for example, involves everything and everybody, and in time of peace any question that is hard to answer is pretty sure to involve money, men, business, and law, and therefore must be of interest to the departments of the Treasury, Labor, Commerce, and Justice, and probably some of the others.

So all members of the Cabinet meet at stated times in a special room adjoining the President's private office in the White House. They sit around a long table, widest in the middle and tapering toward both ends, so the President, sitting at the center, can see and speak easily to each of the ten. Whatever he has in mind he explains to them, and each man, when called upon, gives his advice.

It frequently happens that in addition to the Cabinet members some outsider — some ambassador, or general, or admiral, or other expert — is called in to tell what he knows about some special problem. Some Presidents have had the Vice-President sitting in at all regular meetings.

In this room, around this table, the action of the executive branch of the government is determined; but it is not determined by majority vote. When everyone else has had his say, the final decision rests with the President. If all ten Cabinet members say "yes," and the President says "no," that will be the end of it, for he has the authority. The others are there to give the President advice, not to give him orders. He, and he alone, gives orders.

Of course, it almost never happens that the whole Cabinet is against the President, and when most of them are he sometimes gives up his own idea and accepts their advice. But he doesn't have to. In 1841 President Tyler refused to do so, whereupon the entire Cabinet resigned, except for the Secretary of State, Daniel Webster, and he stayed only long enough to finish a treaty with England on which he was working. This could happen again at any time, although it is most unlikely.

Why, then, isn't this man boss of the whole country, seeing that he can give orders to the greatest of the great officers of state who make up his Cabinet? The reason is that the branch he heads is not the whole government, but only one third of it. The President takes orders from nobody, but neither can he give any to Congress or to the Supreme Court. He cannot give orders to the highest officer of Congress, the Speaker of the House, or to the highest officer of the Supreme Court, the Chief Justice of the United States. Note that this title is Chief Justice *of the United States,* not *of the Supreme Court.*

The President's job is somewhat like that of the general manager of a big business concern. He runs it, in the sense that he sees that its regular work goes on every day, and he can fire anybody who is not doing his job. But the general manager must run the company in the way that the directors say it should be run, and the directors, in their turn, must satisfy the stockholders, for the stockholders have the right to vote them all out of their jobs if they fail to make a success of the business.

Roughly speaking, the President is the general manager of the biggest business on earth, Congress is the board of directors, and the people of the United States are the stockholders. Yet while the government is, in fact, a business, it is very much more than a business, and the President is very much more than the biggest general manager that ever lived.

The way in which he handles the job cannot be described exactly, for every President does it a little differently, and most of them have changed their own first methods a bit after they have worked at it for some time.

There are, however, some things about the job that do not change, no matter who happens to be President. The man in the White House really has five jobs, which are not exactly the same as the five duties described in the Constitution. First, he is head of the executive branch, which means that he must keep the machinery of government running and must keep in touch with the other two branches, Congress and the Supreme Court. Second, he manages foreign affairs, which means that he must keep in touch with other nations, through their ambassadors at Washington and our ambassadors abroad. Third, he is leader of the party that elected him and must arrange party affairs with the other important leaders, some in Congress, some governors of states, some perhaps mere private citizens. Fourth, he is the leader of the people as no other man is, because he and his Vice-President are the only men elected by the people of every state, and he is expected to give them suggestions and ideas on every important subject that comes up. This part of his job has grown tremendously important in recent years. Fifth, he is what is called the ceremonial head of the state. He represents the country. One may say that he *is* the United States when he goes abroad, and when very important people—presidents of other republics, kings of monarchies, and such great officers as the Prime Minister of Great Britain and the head of the Communist party in Russia—come here as guests of the nation.

President Truman once said that this fifth job is in some ways the hardest of all, because it takes so much time and one must be so careful to say and do exactly the right thing.

To arrange all the details that come under these five jobs the President has a number of special assistants. Presidents Roosevelt and Truman had ten, President Eisenhower fourteen, President Kennedy a number that may change at any time. Each of these men looks after a different part of the President's work. They do not do the work; they merely arrange it as conveniently as possible. In addition, there are various secretaries. One, and a very important one, spends his time explaining to newspaper, radio, and other reporters what the President is doing, and usually why he is doing it on that particular day. Another goes through the long list of people who want to see the President every day,

and arranges a time for each one who has important business. If the President saw everybody who wants to come and talk to him, he would never get anything else done. Others go through the newspapers and magazines, as well as the long reports from the various departments, pick out the important parts, and cut them down to a few words that the President can read quickly. Others talk to members of Congress about matters in which the President is interested, or that the Congressmen wish to bring to his attention.

The idea is to arrange the enormous volume of business so that the President will miss nothing important, nor waste his time on matters that someone else can handle as well as he can. But this can't be done by any fixed rule. Nearly every day the President spends some time talking about something that isn't important; he does so because the man who brings it up is important. He may be a Senator who wants the President's help on a small matter that could as well be attended to by a bureau chief. The President listens because some time later he may need the Senator's help on something of great importance, so it is well to keep him in a friendly mood.

The assistant who handles such matters must

know who is important and who is not. If he is really good at his job, he will know how to get rid of the unimportant ones without making them enemies of the President. In the same way, the man who talks to the correspondents must know a great deal about handling news. Every old newspaperman knows that the way you tell a story makes a great deal of difference. Tell it one way, and it may seem to reflect credit on the President. The same facts, told in a different way, may look bad. For instance, let us suppose that the Press Secretary said to the newsmen one morning. "Because the President has to meet the Queen of Sheba at the airport today, the usual meeting of the Cabinet is postponed." That would be a routine item of news, and nobody would think anything of it. But if he said, "The President has dismissed the Cabinet, because he wants to meet the Queen," the statement would have a different sound, although it announced the same fact.

This means that while an assistant to the President may be almost anything else, he must not be stupid. If he speaks or acts stupidly, he will anger some important person who will blame the President for what the assistant did. Sometimes it happens that the President himself makes a mistake. In such cases a smart secretary or special assistant can often smooth things over before much harm is done, but a stupid one will only make matters worse.

One of the most exacting of the duties of these assistants is helping to prepare the President's speeches. Every word that a President utters is carefully studied by his friends and his foes, his friends hoping to help and his foes to hurt him. Therefore, if he says something in a public address that is plainly a mistake, he will never hear the end of it. It is the responsibility of his speech writers to see that there are no mistakes, for the President has to make so many speeches on so many different subjects that he could not possibly check on everything for himself.

Three uniformed men, always in or around the White House, are the military aides representing the Army, the Navy, and the Air Force. The aides are ordinarily of the rank of colonel in the Army or captain in the Navy, but Presidents Roosevelt and Truman had also a chief of staff of the rank of admiral, equivalent to a general in the Army.

Finally, there is a group of men who guard the President against crazy people or criminals who may wish to do him harm. Three Presidents — Lincoln, Garfield, and McKinley — were murdered while in office, and attempts were made to kill three others, Jackson, the second Roosevelt, and Truman. So guards are necessary indeed.

In most monarchies the royal bodyguard is a very showy outfit, usually big men dressed in special and extra-handsome uniforms, and conspicuous wherever the monarch is present. We protect our President in just the other way. The President's guard is drawn from the secret service of the Treasury Department. Most of them are young men, and they are under orders not to be conspicuous. They dress in ordinary clothes, say little, move quietly, and keep their weapons concealed. But they are armed, and they spend many hours practicing how to draw quickly and shoot straight. Whenever and wherever the President appears, they are somewhere close by, paying no attention to him but watching the crowd, ready to jump at the first move by some dangerous person.

The secret service doesn't wait for a new President to move into the White House before beginning to look after him. A man elected in November takes office the following January; but as soon as it

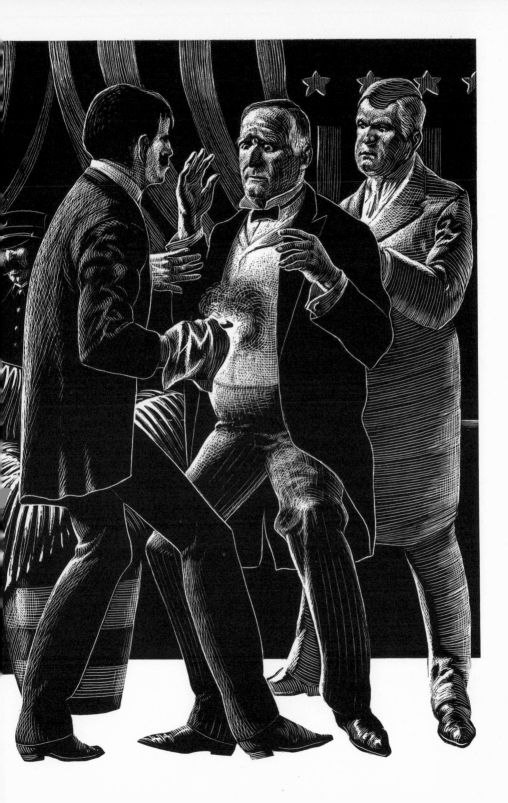

is known who was chosen, the secret service sends men to guard him. Yet with all this care, there is still some danger in being President, or even President-elect. In 1933 an assassin tried to kill Franklin D. Roosevelt before he became President, and did kill the mayor of Chicago, who was standing by Mr. Roosevelt. In 1960 they arrested a man who was making threats against John F. Kennedy after Mr. Kennedy had been elected, but before he took office. And in 1950 two men tried to shoot their way into the house where President Truman was staying while the White House was being repaired. They killed one of the guards, but other guards shot them down before they got beyond the front steps.

Although no two presidents have worked in exactly the same way, it is possible to give a sketch of the President's working day, for certain things have to be done by all of them. Whether he does this job at ten o'clock in the morning and that one at two o'clock in the afternoon, doesn't matter, provided he does both of them sometime during the day.

The President and his family live on the second floor of the White House. The first floor is almost entirely given over to reception rooms, parlors, a banquet room, and other apartments that are more or less public. So the President usually begins his day on the second floor, where he sleeps and where he may have breakfast. With most Presidents this is the time when the doctor makes his daily visit. If nothing seems to be wrong, that takes only a few minutes.

The President may start his day with the morning newspapers, which have been delivered at the White House before he rises, or he may take time in the early morning to be with his family, for he will see little of them during the rest of the day. In any event, he starts his work with the newspapers, for his very first business is to be informed of what is going on.

That doesn't sound very difficult, but actually it is the most difficult thing the President has to do. His information must be as exact and as accurate as is humanly possible. If you and I are a little uncertain about who is fighting whom in some country on the other side of the earth, it doesn't matter much, because nobody expects us to do anything about it. Not so the President of the United States. If anything big happens anywhere in the world, he may have to take a hand in it, in one way or another. Unless he has accurate information he may do the wrong thing, thereby bringing trouble upon the country.

The President must know the truth. If he acts on rumors, gossip, and guesses, as most of us do most of the time, the results will be serious and may be terrible. Unfortunately, he cannot know the exact truth at all times. It is hard to get at the truth about any event that amounts to much, because there are always two opinions as to what really happened, frequently there are twenty, and there may be two hundred. And sometimes they are all wrong.

The best the President can do is to pick out the opinion that seems most closely in line with the known facts; therefore he must have all the known facts, and even then he may be mistaken. When Woodrow Wilson was President, our neighbor nation, Mexico, was in turmoil. Half a dozen factions were each claiming to be the only lawful government. They were fighting among themselves, destroying American lives and property and endangering the peace of the world. The reports from that country were flatly contradictory, even those sent in by men known to be honest. Someone asked the

President how he tried to get at the truth about Mexico, and his answer was, "By balancing lies."

Every President has to do that to some extent in some situations. For that reason, one of the most valuable qualities he can have is good judgment, especially about whom to believe when different people are telling him contradictory things. The ability to tell who is reliable and who is not is something that cannot be learned from books. Some men have it, and some do not. If a man has it in a high degree, he is pretty sure to make a good President; if he has little, or none at all, he is equally sure to make a bad one.

But the finest judgment will go wrong when it is based on false information, so every effort is made to assist the President by giving him all the facts. At a certain time in the morning, usually after he has read the papers, he goes down a corridor from the main part of the White House to his private office in the west wing. In the meantime, many members of his staff have been reading, not only the newspapers, but reports from the various departments, dispatches from ambassadors, teletype reports, and letters from individuals.

These staff men mark passages containing information that the President ought to have, and turn over the marked copies to one secretary chosen for his ability to say much in few words. This man cuts down the marked passages to a line or two containing the bare facts. He reduces the great mass to one typewritten sheet, or two at most, which he lays on the President's desk before his arrival, so that he can read it in the first five minutes he is in the office.

The Appointments Secretary is waiting with a list of people the President is to see and the things he is to do on that day. The President looks it over and gives it his O.K., or makes any changes that he sees fit. Then he is ready for the first of the great number of people who are always clamoring to see him. Or he may turn to the documents he must study and either approve or disapprove, or examine a speech prepared for him, or dictate answers to letters that require his attention and cannot be left to some assistant.

In that case, he will put off seeing people until after lunch; but always, at some time during the day, he must see people, for a great deal of the business of the President cannot be transacted in writing. That is because he is the leader of the nation and others look to him for suggestions and advice. He is a leader, not a dictator. He cannot give orders to the people, nor to their representatives in Congress. When he wants something done outside the executive branch, he must persuade, he cannot command. So he must do a great deal of listening and some arguing, if he is to make a success of his job.

All this is strictly business. In addition, there is a great deal of work that is called ceremonial that must be attended to. Everybody wants the President to lay a cornerstone, or open a new building, or address a convention, or award a prize, or do something else not directly connected with the business of the government. He does as much of this kind of thing as he can, but for every invitation he accepts he must refuse many others.

Then there is the press conference, when the President meets the newspaper, radio, and television reporters assigned to the White House to answer their questions about public business. It is really through this conference that the President does most of his speaking to the country, for anything he says at such a conference is sure to be reported throughout the nation. He has to be extremely careful, for if he says the wrong thing that, too, will be reported widely. Sometimes hostile reporters ask trick questions designed to make him say the wrong thing. For this reason, some Presidents dread the press conference and use it as little as possible; others have found it a very useful instrument by which to explain things to the public.

Then there are all the meetings which the President must attend — Cabinet meetings, committee meetings, interviews with Congressional leaders, and so on.

That is, in general, the kind of thing that goes on in the house that is Number 1600, Pennsylvania Avenue, in the city of Washington.

There is no greater official position in the world than the one held by the master of that house. We Americans believe that there is no other as great, although people of other nations might dispute that. But no one denies that the master of the White House is head of what is certainly the richest and perhaps the strongest country in the world. He commands armed forces that have only one rival. He speaks for a hundred and eighty million people who have attained a very high level of civilization. And he represents a political system that in less than two hundred years has achieved a success never surpassed by any other system in an equal length of time. There can be no denial that, for the time assigned him, he stands among the great lords of the modern world.

But it was not always so. The Presidency in the beginning meant leadership of a small, weak nation, not at the center of civilization, but on its outer rim. It was a nation inspired by a new idea and following a course that many thought was bound to lead to disaster. Washington and his friends could not be certain where they were going; they were acting on what they believed, not on what they knew. They believed that civilized men were capable of governing themselves, but it had not been proved. They were to prove it, and in the course of proving it the Presidency became a different and wholly unexpected thing.

This is something that we seldom take into account, and it sounds somewhat mysterious. But there is really no mystery about it. It was bound to happen. If you trace the way the Presidency has changed, you can see how each new departure grew out of what had gone before and was something that had to be done if self-government were to be made a success. These changes the office has undergone have made Kennedy's job one that Washington could never have dreamed of.

How the Presidency Has Changed

THE PRESIDENT of the United States is much more important than he was intended to be by the men who wrote the Constitution in 1787.

For one thing, the country has grown much faster than they expected, and in the world at large the head of a big nation is always more important than the head of a small one. The Constitution writers knew that as the country grew, the importance of the Presidency would grow with it. They simply did not expect it to grow so fast. In 1800 Jefferson, for instance, thought that we might reach the Pacific by about the year 2050. In fact, California became a state in 1850.

But that isn't all of it. The President is not only more important in the eyes of other countries; here at home he is far more important than the Constitutional Convention meant that he should be. The members of the Convention believed that if any man became as great as the President now is, he would destroy the liberty of the country.

It hasn't happened, as yet. Still, it is not to be denied that it could happen, and some people are very much afraid that it is going to happen. They are so much afraid that in 1951 they adopted an amendment to the Constitution forbidding any man to serve as President for more than ten years. That was because Franklin D. Roosevelt had been elected four times, and his opponents simply couldn't believe that it was because the people really wanted him. They convinced themselves that there was some kind of trickery in it; so when the opposition party got control of Congress in 1946, after Roosevelt's death, they put through this amendment.

It is of doubtful value. Something of the sort was proposed as far back as Washington's day, but Washington said that if the people find a man whom they like, and want to keep him as President, they have a right to do so as long as they please. The Presidency is so strong now, however, that perhaps Washington would not say the same thing today.

Every strong President, including Washington himself, has been accused of plotting to make himself a dictator; yet none has done so. Why not? Part of the answer is that we have never elected a man who loved power more than he loved his country — a man like Napoleon, or Hitler, or Mussolini. But another part is the careful way in which our government was constructed, dividing the powers so that it is almost impossible for any man to gather them all into his own hands.

You can't tell in a sentence why the most powerful ruler in the world has not become a tyrant, as the Constitution makers feared that he might. But if you go back and consider the reasons, one by one, you will find that they hook into each other like the links in a chain, so that at the end it is not hard to understand what happened.

If you ask, as worried people constantly do ask, what is going to come of it all, you are asking a question to which there isn't any answer. We have made mistakes. Some things we have tried worked so badly that we had to drop them and start over again; but others proved to be even better than we had hoped.

If you could count all the American ideas that
have been tried, you would find that there have been
more successful ones than mistakes. So the country
as a whole has been a success. If you will recall three
things: first, what we started with; second, how long
we have been working, and third, where we are
now, you will realize that it has been the greatest
success in history. We started with a small number
of people scattered over a great deal of land. We
have been a nation since 1776, less than two hundred years, which is not very long in the life of a
nation. We are now one of the largest, by far the
richest, and perhaps the most powerful of all the
nations of the world. That is success, and nobody
can deny it.

So our system has been a success up to now. How
much longer we shall succeed nobody knows. For a
nation is not like a house which, once built, may
stand unchanged for a hundred years. A nation is
more like a tree, which keeps on growing until something happens to it. It may be cut down, or struck by
lightning, or killed by blight at any time. But it is
always in one of three states, either growing, or
dying, or dead. It may keep growing for a very long

time; one of the great trees of California may live three or four thousand years. And so may a nation.

Nevertheless, a nation is changing all the time, slowly but steadily, as a sapling changes into a tree. The tall tree is not the sapling that it was, yet it is the same plant. The United States of today is not the United States of 1776, yet it is the same nation. There have been changes in almost every part of it, and it is necessary to understand these changes in order really to know the history of the country.

You have only to look at the way the Constitution is put together, to notice one change. Article I of the Constitution sets up Congress; not until Article II does it get around to the Presidency, and not until Article III to the Supreme Court. That means more than you might think. The men who made the Constitution expected Congress to be the leading branch of the government. If you wonder where they got that idea, you must think of the kind of men they were, and what they knew about governments.

There were fifty-five of them representing the thirteen states at the Constitutional Convention in Philadelphia. Every one of them was a man who

amounted to something in his own state, most of them were known in the other states, and at least two were famous throughout the world. These two were George Washington and Benjamin Franklin. Washington was chosen to preside over the meeting.

All of them had been subjects of the British king for most of their lives and up to 1776 few of them had wished to be anything else. However, when the king's government became so bad that they could no longer bear it, most of them had taken part in throwing it off. Now they were setting up a new government, and their first idea was to avoid the mistakes that had made the British system so bad.

Although the men who made our Constitution disliked King George and especially his ministers, they thought pretty well of the British system in general. What the Americans wished to do was not destroy the whole system of government, but merely improve it to make it fit American conditions.

They agreed that any kind of government, if it is to govern at all, must have three powers—the power to make laws, the power to enforce laws, and the power to decide what the law is in a particular case. These they called the legislative, the executive, and the judiciary.

Then they came up with an idea that some people said was completely crazy, but that turned out to be brilliant. The idea was — split the powers. Set up three branches of government and give one of the powers to each branch. No one would have authority over either of the others, and if one tried to seize all power, the other two would certainly combine to hold it down. They called it a "system of checks and balances," and it was adopted, although many people, including some members of the Convention, feared that it would result in no government at all.

It might have done just that if the Constitution had not been extremely carefully written by some extremely able men. It was the great good luck of the American people that among the fifty-five delegates were a number of the best students of government that the world has ever seen. Two, especially, are remembered as men who probably understood the theory — not the practice — of government as well as any two who have ever lived. They were James Madison of Virginia, and Alexander Hamilton of New York.

Through a long, hot summer in Philadelphia the delegates worked on the Constitution. It was hard work, because they were trying to look ahead and provide for what would happen in the future, as well as for what had already happened; and when people are trying to provide for the future, there are bound to be great differences of opinion. There were such differences in the Convention, and several times they became so violent that they almost broke up the meeting. They would have done so had it not been for Washington, always calm, always steady, when others were getting angry and excited. He got much help from Franklin, also a very wise man, but it was generally agreed that Washington was the man who held the Convention together until it had completed its work.

All the members believed that the country would grow, and as it grew it would need many things that could not be foreseen and provided for at that time. For instance, the Constitution says that there shall be one Supreme Court, but it adds, "and such inferior courts as the Congress may from time to time establish." Congress may set up as many courts as it likes — and it has set up hundreds — provided they are all under the Supreme Court. This is also true of the executive departments; Congress may create new ones as it sees fit, but they must be under the President.

Clearly the Convention expected Congress to take the lead in making whatever changes might be necessary in the government as the country grew, just as Parliament had been taking the lead in England.

They meant to make the Presidency an office of great honor and dignity, the most honorable and dignified in the country, but they were careful not to give it anything like kingly power. They wanted to make the President very grand, but not very great. He was to have no real power over anybody except those persons who broke the law. He was to punish them as the courts directed, and in order that he might be able to do so, he was made supreme commander of all the armed forces, as well as of United States Marshals and other law officers.

The writers of the Constitution intended to make the President what the king of England later became; namely, the head of the state, but not its ruler. The ruler in England today is Parliament, and not even all Parliament, but the House of Commons acting through a committee of its members called the cabinet. In England today the House of Lords can do very little, and the Queen even less; the cabinet and the House of Commons hold all the real power.

*　　　*　　　*

But it didn't work out that way in this country. The President has grown more and more important as time passed. True, the worst that the Constitution makers feared has never happened. No one has tried to make himself a dictator.

Yet it is a fact that if a President today wishes to do so, he can exert more power than the head of any other state except those that do have dictators. He can do it because, first, the people will listen to him as they will listen to no other man, in or out of the government, and, second, because he is the leader of his party and all his party members wish to make him strong. Interestingly enough, not all Presidents have wished to exert the power that is in their hands. It is troublesome. To argue the people into accepting, and the members of Congress into doing, something that needs doing, but that has never been done before, is hard work. It is dangerous work, too, because the moment you start to do something, your enemies can say you are doing the wrong thing and raise a great hubbub about it. As long as you do nothing, there is not much they can say against you.

For this reason, some Presidents have preferred to let Congress take the lead in anything new, and if Congress didn't, nobody did, and nothing was done. A great student of the American system who later became President, Woodrow Wilson, once wrote that there is nothing in law or in morals to stop a President of the United States from being just as big a man as he can be. Wilson might have added that, on the other hand, there is nothing to stop him from being little and of small worth, if that is the kind of man he is.

Those Presidents who, in the past, have preferred to stand back and let Congress take the lead have later been regarded as not much good. If there is nothing much against them, neither is there much for them. They simply didn't count, and now it is hard to remember that they were there at all. The ones whose names are known to every American are the ones who have used and extended the power of the office. Who can remember that Franklin Pierce and Chester A. Arthur and Benjamin Harrison were Presidents of the United States? Who can forget that George Washington and Thomas Jefferson and Abraham Lincoln were?

So there it is. Something has upset the careful balance that the Constitution writers arranged when they split the powers of government three ways.

Furthermore, that something is not what George Washington thought it might be, when in his Farewell Address he warned the American people to watch out for men like Napoleon Bonaparte, who had made himself a dictator.

The Constitution makers believed that the balance of power among the executive, legislative, and judiciary branches of the government would be kept, because each branch would be jealous of the other two. If one tried to snatch some power that belonged to another, the other two would combine to stop it. That was all right, as far as it went. But suppose one branch took unto itself some power that did not belong to either of the others, what then? This was something that they had not provided for, because they did not believe it was possible.

But in a democracy there is a *fourth* power that they knew nothing about. This is the power to start something. It might be called the power of initiative. Most people call it simply leadership, and it is always a one-man power.

It shows up in the simplest things. Suppose in a small neighborhood there is something that needs to be done — a bridge to be built, a new street to

be opened, maybe nothing more than a new lamp-
post to be put up at some dark corner. The people
hold a meeting. But they could sit there forever with
nothing done if some one person didn't get up and
say, "I move we do so-and-so." Then things start.
The meeting may vote for the motion or against it,
but something will be done, one way or another.
The person who makes the motion has assumed the
power of leadership.

This power the Constitution makers placed no-
where, and thereby left an empty place in our system of government. An empty place is a vacuum,
and as the axiom says, "Nature abhors a vacuum."
Nature may or may not, but certainly government
does. If there is power within reach, someone is going to grasp it, and it is because many Presidents
have grasped the power of leadership that the Presidency has become so much greater than the men
who founded the government intended it to be.

George Washington had presided over the meeting in Philadelphia and had taken a large part in
writing the Constitution. If anybody knew what it
meant, he did. He knew that part of the President's
duty was to make treaties with foreign countries,
and he knew that he must do it "by and with the

advice and consent of the Senate." He thought those
words meant that the Senators should advise the
President how they wanted the treaty made and
that he should then go ahead and make it accord-
ingly.

As soon as he became President, he found that
the treaty of peace made with Great Britain to end
the Revolutionary War in 1783 had left a great
many loose ends that ought to be tied up. Our mer-
chant ships and fishing boats were always having
disputes with the British. It was hard to do business
with Great Britain when nobody knew exactly what
his rights were. Businessmen, fishermen, and sea-
men were constantly complaining, and it was plainly
necessary to get things straightened out. So the Secretary of State and the British minister talked things
over, and our minister in London talked to the British foreign minister. Washington made up his mind
as to what ought to be done, and then he went to the
Senate to get its advice and consent.

But did he get it? He did not! He had worked
hard on his speech to the Senate. He had explained
very clearly just what he proposed to do, and why.
Of course, if the Senate had what it thought was a
better plan, he was willing to hear it. But if the Sen-

ate had nothing better to offer, then he asked its consent to go ahead.

The Senate, however, talked and talked, and hemmed and hawed, and argued and disputed, and couldn't make up its mind about anything. It wouldn't say yes, and it wouldn't say no. In the meantime, the Secretary of State and the British minister were waiting, business was getting more snarled up every day, complaints kept pouring in, and Washington's temper — he had a fierce one — was rising higher and higher. Finally he told his men to go ahead and make the treaty. When it was drawn up, he sent it to the Senate saying, not in these words but to this effect, "Here it is. Take it or leave it!" In the end the Senators took it, but Washington was so furious over the whole business that he swore he would never again ask the Senate for its advice and consent before a treaty was made. He never did. And every President since has followed the same course; when a treaty is necessary, he goes ahead and makes it. The Senate can accept or reject it, but it plays no part in making it.

Right then and there the Presidency began to change from what the Constitution makers intended it to be. It was not that Washington wanted to change it; it was simply that as President he had to get things done. He couldn't wait forever while the Senate dawdled.

Thus Washington added to the power of the Presidency, and not everybody was pleased. The Constitution was not adopted until it had been agreed that certain amendments, usually called the Bill of Rights, would be added to it immediately to prevent the power of the central government from becoming too great. The tenth of these amendments says that any powers not specifically granted to the federal government or forbidden to the states are "reserved to the states or to the people."

That amendment has never had much effect in halting the increase of the power of the central government, and especially of the Presidency. There are two opinions as to the reason for its failure. One is that the tenth amendment never worked, because it never could be made to work. According to this opinion, power cannot be reserved. If it isn't exercised, it disappears. The other opinion is that a few strong and ambitious men have usurped the reserved powers and wrongfully taken them from the states and the people.

To support this second opinion, it is often pointed

out that the power of the Presidency has not grown steadily and evenly. Under some Presidents it has not advanced at all, while under others it has taken great strides. This does suggest that the strong and ambitious may have taken unto themselves so much power that they have undermined the whole American system, so it is worth while to examine them and their records.

The
Strong Presidents

SINCE THE RATIFICATION of the Constitution, thirty-four individuals have been President of the United States, but they were not all equally important. You can prove that to yourself simply by trying to name them all. You will find it hard to do.

Since Washington there have been six, however, whom everybody remembers, because under each of them the Presidency changed sharply. Each of them in his own time was accused of changing it deliberately, simply because he wanted to. Each was called a wicked man, who wished to be a dictator. But the fact is that each was a great man, who picked up power because nobody else was using it and it was necessary that it be used.

There were other strong men under whom the

Presidency expanded, but not in such a startling way. So if we look at the record of each of the six, we can see how the office has changed since George Washington's time. The six, and the time during which each was President, are:

Thomas Jefferson, 1801-1809

Andrew Jackson, 1829-1837

Abraham Lincoln, 1861-1865

Theodore Roosevelt, 1901-1909

Woodrow Wilson, 1913-1921

Franklin D. Roosevelt, 1933-1945

Three of them served for eight years each, Lincoln for four and a fraction, Theodore Roosevelt for seven and a fraction, and Franklin D. Roosevelt for twelve and a fraction. All but the first Roosevelt were elected twice, and the second Roosevelt was elected four times. Theodore Roosevelt was elected after having served three years as President, because President McKinley was murdered and Roosevelt was his Vice-President. It is clear, therefore, that all were liked by the people, even though their enemies denounced them, and that the changes they made in the Presidency seemed to the country to be right and necessary.

When he was alive people felt about George

Washington as Americans have felt about no other man. There was nobody like him, and when the time came to choose the first President not a single electoral vote was cast for anybody else. By the end of his first term of four years he had made a few enemies, but not enough to count for one electoral vote, so again he got them all.

But Washington was not a vain man, and he never realized how high he stood in the people's minds. He took it for granted that other Presidents would be able to stand, and should stand, as he did, above all the quarrels and disputes over how the government should be run. The second President, John Adams, tried to follow Washington's example, but he couldn't do it. Although he was a good man and in some ways a great man, John Adams was no Washington.

In a very short time he was involved in disputes. One of the most important men in politics at that time, Alexander Hamilton, turned against Adams, and some men that the President thought his best friends, including certain members of his Cabinet, began to pay more attention to Hamilton than to Adams. They wouldn't help him. At times they wouldn't even carry out his orders, and they were constantly running to Hamilton with tales about the President. They made his life a burden and prevented his doing a good job, so at the end of four years he was defeated for re-election.

The third President was Thomas Jefferson. He had watched what happened to Adams and had made up his mind that it wasn't going to happen to him. He saw that Adams' mistake was failing to make certain that his chief assistants should be men who thought pretty much the way he thought. If they had agreed on the main things, then disagreements on minor matters would never have broken up the administration. When Adams became President he kept part of Washington's Cabinet in office. It was a mistake. Having been appointed by Washington, those men felt that they owed nothing to Adams, and so they were not diligent about carrying out his plans. Sometimes, indeed, they opposed them.

Jefferson took note, and when he became President, he made a clean sweep of the Cabinet, putting in men whom he felt he could trust, since they were of his own mind on most things. All of them were able men, quite as good as those in Adams' Cabinet, but that wasn't what made them a new kind of cabinet. The thing that set them apart was that every man of them agreed with Jefferson's main ideas as to what the government ought to be. Both Washington and Adams had felt that the first and most important task before the new nation was to make sure that it would last, for at the time when they held the Presidency it seemed very doubtful that the United States could endure for more than a few years. With this in mind, they did everything they could to make the federal government as strong as possible. This is what gave them, and those who thought like them, the name of Federalists.

Alexander Hamilton agreed with them, but he went further. It was his idea that the best way to make the federal government strong was to make it wealthy. Therefore, he favored doing everything that would encourage those Americans who knew how to make money, and that, of course, made all the rich men in the country strong for Hamilton.

Jefferson did not want the country to remain poor, but he wanted the wealth to be pretty evenly distributed, so that everybody would have something, but nobody would have a great deal. He came to feel that the danger of the country's losing its independence was less than the danger of the citizens' losing their liberty. The way to prevent this loss was to oppose Hamilton and his friends, and the way to do that was to organize his own friends and get them to work together. So he did, and that was when our political parties began. Since the Hamiltonians had taken the name of Federalists, the Jeffersonians looked around for a name that would mean the opposite. At first they called themselves Republicans. After a few years, not satisfied with that, they changed their name to Democratic-Republicans, and finally to Democrats. The Federalist party went to pieces after the War of 1812, but the Hamiltonians did not become Jeffersonians; they organized a new party under the name of Whig. When that disintegrated, most of them joined a third party that had picked up the original Jeffersonian name, Republican. But through all the changes of names, the Democratic party has always looked upon Jefferson as its founder, and the Republican party has looked upon Hamilton as its founder.

So the President became a party man, as Washington had feared he might, but the evils that Washington dreaded have not followed. There are many reasons for this, the chief being that the American parties are very loosely held together. Many an American calls himself a Democrat or a Republican although he frequently votes for the men and measures of the other party. This puzzles foreigners and leads many of them to say that we have no parties at all. But we do, and the President as leader of his party is much more powerful than he was when he stood alone above all parties.

At the same time Jefferson also boldly extended the power of the Presidency by making the Louisiana Purchase. He had the choice of moving fast, or not moving at all. But to move fast he had to take action that, if it did not exactly break the Constitution, certainly bent it pretty badly.

In 1783, when the original peace treaty was signed with Great Britain, almost all the people of the United States lived east of the Appalachian mountain system. By far the greater part of the people lived east of the Blue Ridge and the Allegheny ranges. The treaty, however, fixed the western boundary of the new country at the Mississippi River, and most people thought it would be a hundred years before we settled all that country. But within twenty years it was already filling up, and by 1803 American trade down the Ohio and the Mississippi Rivers was becoming important.

Now the mouth of the Mississippi River had never been held by Great Britain. Part of the time it was owned by Spain, part of the time by France, but never by England. Thus it became a bottleneck for American trade up and down the river. Whenever the governor of that territory, whether French or Spanish, chose to do so, he could make an extra charge for use of the port of New Orleans to transfer goods from the flatboats, which came down the river, to ocean-going ships, which crossed the Gulf of Mexico and the Atlantic. If the governor was feeling unusually vicious, he could stop the trade altogether.

Just before 1803 Napoleon, already dictator and soon to make himself emperor of France, fought and whipped Spain and took from her all the territory then called Louisiana, which meant both sides of the mouth of the Mississippi and nearly all the land on the western bank south of Canada and east of California. Of course, nobody knew then exactly where the southern limit of Canada or the eastern limit of California was.

Then word came to Jefferson, very secretly, that Napoleon was thinking of war against England, and needed money so badly that he might be willing to sell New Orleans to the United States. Jefferson immediately called in several leaders in Congress and told them, and these leaders persuaded Congress to vote to give two million dollars to the President for a purpose not stated. In spite of the hush-hush way it was done, word soon got around that he was trying to buy New Orleans.

When the men we sent to make the deal arrived in Paris, however, they were told that Napoleon had suddenly changed his mind. He would not sell New Orleans for two million, but he would sell all of Louisiana for fifteen million. It was a tremendous bargain, but when the word came to this country Congress had already adjourned. It would take weeks to get it together again, and in the meantime Napoleon might change his mind once more. Should Jefferson wait until he got authority to act, and thereby risk missing the greatest bargain ever offered the country, or should he act without authority? He decided to act, and the deal was made.

Jefferson's first idea was that he should go to Congress and ask for what was called "an act of amnesty," that is, a sort of pardon for having exceeded his authority. But when the American people realized he had bought for them nearly a third of a continent for something less than three cents an acre, they were delighted. The idea that a man needed a pardon for doing such a fine thing seemed to them to be flat nonsense. Nobody in Congress ever proposed an act of amnesty, and nothing more was said about it.

Nevertheless, the Louisiana Purchase extended the power of the Presidency. Without making any change in the Constitution as it was written, we agreed that when the President sees a chance to do something which he is certain will be of great benefit to the country, he has all the authority he needs to do it unless it is expressly forbidden by the Constitution. Half a century later President Johnson acted on this theory in obtaining Alaska, and half a century after that President Theodore Roosevelt obtained the Panama Canal Zone in similar fashion.

As the people saw it, the question was not one of law, but of plain common sense. Certain things the Constitution says the President shall not do—declare war, for instance, or give someone a title of nobility, such as knight or baron—and if he does what is forbidden, he may be impeached. But the Constitution itself was established "to promote the general welfare"; those very words are in the preamble. Therefore, if anything will promote the general welfare it cannot be contrary to the Constitution. So, at least, they argued at the time of the Louisiana Purchase, and they would not hear of giving Jefferson a pardon for doing a great thing.

Here, then, are the two most striking changes that the Presidency underwent in Jefferson's time—the admission that the President always has power to promote the general welfare, even though the Constitution doesn't say so, and the organization of a party to help him get things done. They added greatly to the power of the Presidency, yet did not take anything from either Congress or the Supreme Court.

Skip over the next three Presidents. Although they were able men and did some important things, the Presidency did not change much until the seventh man, Andrew Jackson, held the office.

This man was of a different type from any of those who had been President before him. Except for Washington, all the others were college men, two from Harvard, two from William and Mary, one from Princeton. All were from well-to-do families and Washington was very rich. That is to say, they were what in this country we call aristocrats.

But Jackson came up the hard way. His father died before he was born, and his mother when he was only fourteen. He was very poor, and worked as a saddle maker until he got together enough money to study law. Then he went from North Carolina over the mountains into Tennessee, which was then the wild West. It was a tough country, in which only tough men could last, and Jackson lasted. He had gun fights and knife fights and plain fist-and-skull fights. He was shot several times, he was stabbed, he was beaten, but nearly always the other man came off worse. He fought a duel with one man who was regarded as a dead shot, and he killed the fellow, although he took a bullet in the shoulder himself. Still he was an honest man, as well as a bold one, so the people made him first a judge, and then a Senator. While he was still a judge they made him commander of the state militia, and in the War of 1812 he won a great battle at New Orleans—almost our only great victory in that war.

They tried to make him President in 1824 and

barely missed it. Some said he was cheated out of the election. In 1828 they tried again, and this time he won in a landslide.

Now the men who made the Constitution, although they were for freedom, did not believe that the common people had education enough and sense enough to choose a good man for President. The people could recognize a good man when he was a neighbor and they knew him by sight, but what did they know about a man from some distant state? In the opinion of the Constitution makers, nothing, or certainly not enough to judge him accurately. So they arranged to have the people choose someone whom they knew to be an honest man and make him what was called an elector. Then the electors in each state would meet and vote for a man they thought should be President. The votes would be reported to Congress and counted there, and the man who had the most would be declared President.

But the people in all the states had at least heard of Jackson and most of them liked him. So when it came time in 1828 to choose the electors, the people asked them, "Will you promise, if chosen, to vote for Andrew Jackson?" Those who promised got the votes. Thus, Jackson came to Washington elected by the people and nobody else, and he regarded himself as the people's man.

Certainly each member of Congress was elected by some people, but not by all the people. Each member of the House of Representatives represented a district, but the people of the next district had no say in choosing him. Each Senator represented a state, but the adjoining states could not vote for or against him. Only the President and Vice-President were chosen by all the people of all the states.

Up to 1828 it was not the custom to allow the people even to nominate the candidate of their party. Instead, the party members of Congress met in a caucus and selected the candidate. But Jackson was nominated by the people acting through their state legislatures; and when he won, that finished the caucus.

We still vote for electors, and the electors still vote for the President. But ever since Jackson's day, we know how the elector is going to vote before we choose him, which comes to the same thing as voting directly for the President—except, of course, when some elector goes back on his word, which happens occasionally.

Then in 1832 the Jackson party, by this time known as the Democrats, called a great national convention instead of the caucus. They would not even hold it in Washington, where Congress met. They gathered in Baltimore and there declared that Jackson should be the candidate of the party again, and that Martin Van Buren should be the candidate for Vice-President. They were elected, and candidates have been chosen by national conventions ever since.

Jackson's administration was one of the most exciting in American history, perhaps the most exciting one in which there was no great war. For while there were no military battles, one tremendous political row followed another as long as he was President. At the start his enemies made the mistake of thinking that he was no more than an ignorant countryman, who could easily be fooled by the smart gentlemen who were running things in Washington. It was a bad error, for while it was true that Jackson had had very little schooling, he had learned a great deal outside of school. On the wild frontier he had discovered how to manage men so as to persuade them to do what he wanted done. He knew more about that than anyone else in Washington, and that is the kind of knowledge a President needs.

If his enemies had known this, they would never have tried to run over him. But they didn't know it, so there was a roaring battle over the Bank of the United States (Jackson destroyed it) and another over the tariff (Jackson finally had his way there, too). Then South Carolina ventured to declare a law of the United States no law (null) in South Carolina, and Jackson almost started a civil war then and there, and would have if they had not given up nullification.

These fights were so long and loud, and over so many different things, that at the time few people noticed how Jackson was changing the Presidency. They thought that he was changing it into a dictatorship, but what he was actually doing was compelling the little group in Washington who had been running the country to pay some attention to the will of the people. Jackson felt that he represented the people back home and should protect them against the political machine.

The makers of the Constitution had not seen it so. They had the idea that the President should represent the nation to the rest of the world, and at home should represent the national dignity and power. They expected Congress to represent the people. But it didn't work out that way. Because of the way in which they were elected, each member of Congress represented a district, or, if he were a Senator, one state. None of them would, or could, represent the whole people.

But the people felt that they needed a man of their own choice in the government and they made the President their man. This was a tremendous change in the Presidency, and one that Jackson greatly encouraged and assisted.

When power to nominate candidates was taken from the caucus and assumed by the party in its national convention, many said it was usurpation. But the Constitution says not a word about the caucus, nor about any other method of nominating candidates. It was another power vacuum. By setting up the caucus, Congress moved into it first. But the people, led by Jackson, threw Congress out and took the power themselves. Since our theory is that all power belongs to the people in the first place, whatever they take back to themselves cannot be called usurpation. If you must have a word for it, it is re-sumption.

After Jackson, we can skip over the next eight Presidents, for none of them did much to change the Presidency. In fact, none of them did much of anything except the eleventh, Polk, who seized California and then made Mexico sell it to us for the same price paid Napoleon for Louisiana—fifteen million dollars.

The sixteenth President was Abraham Lincoln, one so great in other respects that what happened to the Presidency under him is often hardly noticed. Lincoln saved the Union and destroyed slavery. After that, anything else he did seems scarcely worth mentioning.

Nevertheless, he too moved into a power vacuum, and a very large one. The Constitution had made the President commander in chief of the Army and Navy at all times, and of all armed forces, including the militia, in time of war; but it had not given him many other war powers. Neither had it given them to anyone else. It had not seemed necessary and is not, in fact, necessary in a small, limited war.

The war that broke out in 1861, however, was a desperate one, much more so than many of us can now realize. We have raised far greater armies since, and fought bigger battles; but in the Civil War Americans fought Americans on American soil, and the combat was fiercer than any we have undergone, before or after. In the Civil War every fifth man was killed in battle or died in the Army. In the Second World War, a far bigger contest, only about one man in twenty lost his life. In proportion to the numbers engaged, the Civil War was four times as bloody. The national government came nearer losing it, too, for at least twice Confederate troops came within sight of Washington on the Maryland side.

This means that it was the kind of war in which every weakness of the government was bound to show up. One weakness in ours was that, except for the actual command of the troops, few wartime powers had been given to anyone. So Lincoln took them. As a matter of fact, he took too many, and after the war was over Congress enacted laws to make sure that some of them should not be taken again. But most of the powers that Lincoln assumed were so clearly necessary that they have remained in the hands of the President ever since.

They are very great. Indeed, they are so great that in time of war the President of the United States is almost a dictator. But what can you do about it? In time of war, speed is of the utmost importance. If you don't move fast, the enemy will be all over you before you know it and you will not have a chance. But you can't move fast unless somebody can give the order to move, and give it without hesitation.

As one famous American, Alfred E. Smith, said many years later, in time of war "we adjourn the Constitution." So during the Civil War, Lincoln gave the orders, although the Constitution had given him no power to do so, and in every war since every President has done likewise.

Of course, many people called Lincoln a dictator and a tyrant, for in his hands the Presidency did acquire far greater power than it had ever had before. More than that, it was not power over such things as the Bank of the United States, nullifying legislatures, or treaties made with foreign nations. It was power over the individual citizen, power over you and me. When war is raging, it is extremely dangerous for anyone to defy an order of the President of the United States. It almost certainly means going to jail, and it may mean being put to death.

❈   ❈   ❈

Skip over ten Presidents more. (Nine, really, because Grover Cleveland is counted twice. He was
first elected as the twenty-second President, then
after four years he was defeated and another man
was elected as the twenty-third. After another four
years, Cleveland made a comeback and was elected
as the twenty-fourth.) We pass over the nine not
because nothing happened in their time, but because the Presidency didn't change much under
them. But it did change, very decidedly, under
Theodore Roosevelt.

It is not easy to explain exactly how it changed
while this man was in the White House. For instance, he "took" the Panama Canal Zone; he came
in to make peace when Russia and Japan were
at war, although we were not mixed up in the quar-
rel; and he sent the battle fleet around the world to
impress other nations with our power. In such things
as these many Americans thought that he was acting
as no other President had ever acted, and so was
changing the Presidency.

But that is not correct. Although Roosevelt himself used the word "took" in speaking of Panama, he
didn't simply take it; he bought it, paying—counting

forty millions to the old French canal company and
ten to the Republic of Panama — more than three
times as much as Jefferson had paid for Louisiana
or Polk for California. As for persuading Russia and
Japan to make peace, many other Presidents had
tried to stop or prevent wars, especially in Central
and South America, so that was nothing new. As
for sending the fleet around the world, President
Fillmore sent a squadron under Commodore Perry
to impress Japan in 1854. In all these acts Roosevelt
was only doing what at least one President had done
before him. Yet historians agree that when he left
the White House the Presidency was different from
what it had been when he entered it.

What made the difference was Roosevelt's belief
that it was the duty of the President to tell the
people not only what he thinks is the smart thing to
do, but also what is the right thing. More than any
preceding President he spoke and wrote about what
is right and what is wrong. At the time few noticed
that he was adding a new duty to the Presidency.
But he was. He was making it the duty of the President to denounce any kind of rascality, whether it
was in the government, in business, or anywhere
else. For instance, the President, who was an ardent

amateur naturalist, noticed that some people were writing what he considered a lot of lies about birds and wild animals in magazine articles. So he spoke out loudly against these "nature fakers."

That is one small and not very important example of the kind of thing he did. Much more significant was the way he went after men who were taking an unfair advantage in business and men who were playing dirty politics. Most of the earlier Presidents had felt that if they kept their own hands clean, that was enough. Roosevelt didn't think it was enough. He thought the President should stir up the people against evil men and evil deeds wherever he found them. This brought people to look upon the President as, to some extent, the moral as well as the political leader of the nation. And this changed the Presidency more than any of Theodore Roosevelt's acts.

The next President whom nobody forgets was Woodrow Wilson. So much happened to the Presidency during his time that even now, forty years later, we don't know exactly what it all means. It was not that Wilson planned any great changes. When he became President, in 1913, his purpose was to carry forward and perhaps improve on the kind of work that Theodore Roosevelt had done. In his first two years in office, he did, in fact, put through many laws that made both business and politics fairer and more honest.

But before the end of Wilson's second year, the whole imperial system, by which most of the world had been governed for at least three hundred years, blew up in the First World War. From that time on, neither Wilson nor the American people had much control over events. The President and the nation were like men caught in a hurricane; instead of going where they chose, they had to scramble to keep from being blown away. Their first idea was to keep out of the war, but they might as well have tried to keep out of an earthquake. The whole world system was falling down, and nobody could keep out of it.

In the midst of the uproar, however, Wilson conceived one great idea. Of course, it was not his alone; many others held it, but Wilson was the one head of a powerful state who accepted it fully and meant to act on it. By the time the war ended, in fact, his was by long odds the most powerful government on earth, for all the other big ones, Japan excepted, had been terribly weakened by the fighting.

The idea was that since the old system had collapsed, reasonable men in all nations must get together and build a new one that would be stronger. Wilson thought that the fatal weakness of the old system was that so many of the imperial governments were not, as our Declaration of Independence puts it, "deriving their just powers from the consent of the governed." This made him determined that the new system should be based on that consent.

You can't understand what has happened to the Presidency, however, if you consider Wilson by himself. Along with him you have to take a look at the sixth unforgettable President, Franklin D. Roosevelt, for they really were a team. At the time of his death the second Roosevelt was trying to finish what Wilson had started, for during Roosevelt's time what was left of the old system fell down with an even more terrific crash in the Second World War. So in considering Wilson it is necessary always to bear in mind that his story runs on into that of Roosevelt.

Shortly after Wilson's first election, he announced that he proposed to be the leader of the Democratic party as well as President. But every strong President had been the leader of his party, so that was nothing new. By the end of the First World War, however, it became plain that he was going to have to lead a great deal more than the United States and the Democratic party, whether he wanted to or not. By that time four once-great empires — Germany, Austria-Hungary, Russia, and Turkey—had crashed. The British empire was badly hurt, and France — not exactly an empire, but the holder of many colonies—was even more hurt. The United States, however, had been merely stung, not crippled, by the war. If anyone were to lead, it had to be this country, for none of the others had the strength.

So Wilson undertook to lead, not the Democratic party only, and not this country only, but all the free nations. That, of course, made a tremendous change in the Presidency, and a great many Americans could not see the need. Some declared that the League of Nations, Wilson's plan for bringing together reasonable men to prevent any more wars, was nothing but a scheme on Wilson's part to make himself a sort of President of the world. So this country refused to join the League, and without what was then the strongest nation in the world it never had much of a chance.

Perhaps it never had a chance anyhow. There were a great many people, especially in Europe, who

could not believe that the imperial system was really finished, and they, of course, did not consider the League necessary. Russia, having gone Communist, was not allowed to join. Four years after the end of the war Benito Mussolini, having seized the government of Italy, repudiated the whole idea of a League of Nations and started to build an empire more tyrannical than those that had fallen. Eleven years after that, Adolf Hitler, in Germany, beat Mussolini at his own game. The League of Nations was not strong enough to stop either of them, and perhaps it could not have stopped them even if we had been a member.

As to that, nobody knows. All we do know is that Hitler and Mussolini built two systems far worse than the former empires. The result was the Second World War, which finished the empires completely and left only two really strong nations in the world, the United States and Russia.

In the meantime, nineteen years passed and the United States had three more Presidents. None of them did anything about Wilson's idea, nor did any of them do anything else that made much change in the Presidency.

Then came the second Roosevelt. At first he had
his hands full with affairs at home. The First World
War had not only broken down the imperial political
system, it had shattered many of the old ways of
doing business, especially finance, the system of
making payments for goods and services. Things
were in such a snarl that nobody knew how to
straighten them out. The snarl got worse and worse
until, about 1929, the whole system crashed. Business slowed down so much, that by the end of 1932
it had very nearly stopped altogether. In November
of that year Franklin D. Roosevelt was elected
President.

Not since Lincoln, in 1861, had a new President
had such a mess on his hands. The day before
Roosevelt was inaugurated every bank in New York
closed its doors, after most of the banks elsewhere
had already closed. On that day the whole country
was literally bankrupt, and the new President's ef-
forts to get things started again gave him little time
to think about other matters.

The second Roosevelt was a cousin of the first,
and Franklin had a great admiration for Theodore,
although the first had been a Republican and the
second was a Democrat. In some ways they were

much alike. The second Roosevelt didn't talk about morality as much as the first, but he believed in it quite as strongly; and, like the first, he believed that the President ought to lead the country whenever and wherever it needed leadership.

In 1933 the crisis was in business, not in politics, so to business Roosevelt first turned his attention. He called Congress into special session, and in what is called the Hundred Days (actually, ninety-nine, but they picked up the phrase because it had been well-known since Napoleon made his second try at empire and lasted exactly a hundred days) the two Houses passed more laws relating to business than the country had seen in any previous year.

They passed a good many other laws, too, most of them designed to keep people from starving to death before business picked up again. Roosevelt seized the chance to get done a great many things that had been neglected for years, and some people thought they saw in these activities a great change in the Presidency. But the only real change was that the panic enabled Roosevelt to move much faster than most Presidents. Practically all the things he did had been proposed years before he was elected, but the government had never got around to doing them. The proof of that is that although the new laws were put through with great speed, not a single important thing done at that time has been undone by later administrations.

Many people disliked what happened during Roosevelt's administrations, and when men dislike anything they are slow to believe that it is necessary. So when Roosevelt insisted on passing laws to help the people during the depression, his enemies believed that he was doing it because he wanted to, not because he had to. They hated him more bitterly than any President since Wilson, perhaps since Lincoln, had been hated. Sometimes Roosevelt made mistakes, and when he did his enemies would never believe it was a mistake, they always thought it a deliberate crime.

On the other hand, Roosevelt's friends — and they were the majority — loved him with an intensity not approached since Lincoln. What Roosevelt's enemies thought was criminal, the friends thought was magnificent. To a large extent both were wrong. No man can manage history. The great statesman is the one who understands the meaning of events that he cannot control and leads his nation safely around traps that few see except the statesman.

Toward the end of Roosevelt's second term, war broke out in Europe again, and again the American people found themselves caught in a storm from abroad that made all their troubles at home seem of little account. According to tradition, Roosevelt should have retired in 1940, but with the war raging in Europe he decided to ask the people to elect him a third time, and they did so with a whoop. They elected him a fourth time in 1944, but he barely began that term. He died three months after his inauguration.

Thus Harry S. Truman, the man who had been elected Vice-President in 1944, suddenly became not merely President of the United States, but leader of all the free nations that had survived the war. It was a position that no earlier President had held. Roosevelt and Wilson had been war leaders, but at the end of World War I Wilson's followers left him, and Roosevelt didn't live to see the end of World War II. Truman was the first American President to be looked on as the spokesman for free men, not only here but wherever freedom exists.

This was because Roosevelt and Churchill, Prime Minister of Great Britain, had agreed that as soon as the war was won they would have another try at what Wilson had failed to do — bringing together reasonable men of all nations, to prevent any more world wars. This new effort they called the United Nations. It was formally organized in San Francisco in 1945, a few weeks after Roosevelt's death. Most of the other nations, even Soviet Russia, went along with the idea, because there seemed nothing else to do.

When Truman became President, he found himself head of a nation that was by far the richest, and probably the strongest, in an organized society of nations. Although he could not command other nations, he had the power to lead them.

Yet Mr. Truman would be the last man to claim that he seized this power, nor did Roosevelt seize it for him. It was thrust upon the Presidency by the way things happened. So it has always been. The people who accused Washington, Jefferson, Jackson, Lincoln, and Wilson of being tyrants and usurpers and would-be dictators were talking nonsense. They were patriots, who did what they believed to be best for the country under new conditions. They were not always right, but they were always loyal, and none ever dreamed of making himself a sort of King of America.

They did deliberately, however, take the leadership that the Constitution had not given any of the three branches of government. It is clear that this was done by their own choice, because not all Presidents have done it. Some have shrunk from the responsibility of starting anything, and if they chose not to do so, nobody could compel them. The man in the White House can let things ride and leave leadership to anyone who can get it, if he is that kind of man, and some Presidents have been that kind. They chose not to lead, with the result that nothing new was done during their administrations.

The fact that the Presidency has changed greatly from Washington to Kennedy brings up what seems to be, but is not, a fair question. The question is, has the change been for the better or for the worse? It is not fair, because it has no answer. It is like asking, "Which do you like better, oysters or pie?" There is no answer to that because the answer depends on the time, the place, and your own mood. Oysters and pie cannot be compared with each other, nor can the Presidency as it was to begin with and the Presidency as it is today.

But this much we can say confidently: whether a

President is a good one or a poor one does not depend on whether he writes with a goose quill or a typewriter. It does not depend on whether he has one secretary or fifty. It does not depend on whether he leads one nation or all free people in all the world. It depends on whether or not he can and will lead.

If you don't want to believe that ability to lead is the most valuable quality a President can have, you should not take the word of this book for it. There are, in fact, some pretty good reasons for not wanting to believe it. Like every good thing, the ability to lead can be abused, and when it is abused it gives rise to terrible evils. Three of the greatest leaders of the twentieth century were Adolph Hitler, Benito Mussolini, and Joseph Stalin. Hitler and Mussolini led their countries to ruin, and Stalin led his into a tyranny that made America shudder.

It could happen here. A wicked man, or a crazy man, given the power that a President of the United States has, especially the power of leadership, could bring upon this country so much trouble that it could not be measured. Thus far, we have never elected such a man, but that is no proof that we never will. By the time a man has become prominent enough to be seriously considered for President, he is pretty well-known to most of the voters. If there is anything seriously wrong with his character it always shows up in his acts, and the people do not vote for a man known to be a downright crook.

But they have elected some who, although personally honest, were not much good, which proves that the people's judgment is not always perfect. They can be and they have been fooled about a man's ability, and sometime they may be fooled about one's honesty. This means that the final test of our country's safety is the good sense of the voters, which means you and me.

That is a rather grim thought, for if we are honest with ourselves, we know that it isn't easy to judge fairly and calmly when excited people all around us are shouting contradictory advice in our ears. But this danger is the price of freedom. It is now, it always has been, and it always will be dangerous. to be free. Grim or not, it is the truth, and it has to be faced.

No country, and most certainly no democracy, can last long without leadership. But in a democracy the people choose the leadership, so when all is said and done, they are responsible for it, whether it is good or bad.

It is a serious thing to be an American citizen, a free man in a free country, and it is more serious than ever now, when this country has become so strong that other free countries expect it to furnish leadership to them. For if we should follow foolish or wicked men, we should not only ruin ourselves, but drag down the other free nations with us. It is no wonder that some people are not gratified, but horrified, by the power that the Presidency has today, and are anxious to cut it down.

That is not the way to safety. All history shows that we have never been safer than when some wise and honest leader, usually a great President, was boldly urging us to do whatever was necessary to meet some new peril. Even when war resulted, we were actually safer than we were without leadership in time of peace. Therefore, intelligent votes mean more to national defense than armed forces.

So far, we have done reasonably well, although a good deal less than perfectly well. We could do better, and there always are men doing their best to see that we shall do better. Nearly a century and a half ago one of the wisest Americans, Thomas Jefferson, wrote to John Adams when both were old men, no longer in public life, recalling the dangers and difficulties they had faced together when they and the republic were young. Again and again it had seemed that all was lost, that the new nation must go down. Yet every time the danger passed, they hardly knew how, and the changes that seemed to be ruinous turned out to be good. Jefferson reminded Adams of that, and then added a remark about the future of America that seems an appropriate one today: "And so we have gone on, and so we shall go on, puzzled and prospering beyond example in the history of man."

Afterword

On November 22, 1963, after this book was in print, John Fitzgerald Kennedy, thirty-fifth President of the United States, having gone to make a speech in the city of Dallas, Texas, was shot and killed there, and the Vice-President, Lyndon B. Johnson, became the thirty-sixth President.

This kind of murder is called an assassination because the killer did not hate the victim, whom he had never met, but hated the victim's office and his country. He had the idea that he could somehow damage the Presidency and the United States by murdering the President, which made his act not only dreadful but silly.

The crime gave the country a terrible shock, because President Kennedy was young, brave, handsome, active, and cheerful, just the kind of leader that the people have always loved. But the Presidency is not touched by the murder of a President. Four times it has happened, and every time the Vice-President has become President and has gone straight ahead with whatever the dead President had been doing. The crime at Dallas really did nothing except fill the country with sorrow and anger.

The Presidency goes on. It is changed by a change in the course of history, but never by the act of a madman or a traitor.

Presidents of the United States

	President	Term of Office
1.	GEORGE WASHINGTON	1789–1797
2.	JOHN ADAMS	1797–1801
3.	THOMAS JEFFERSON	1801–1809
4.	JAMES MADISON	1809–1817
5.	JAMES MONROE	1817–1825
6.	JOHN QUINCY ADAMS	1825–1829
7.	ANDREW JACKSON	1829–1837
8.	MARTIN VAN BUREN	1837–1841
9.	WILLIAM HENRY HARRISON	1841–1841
10.	JOHN TYLER	1841–1845
11.	JAMES K. POLK	1845–1849
12.	ZACHARY TAYLOR	1849–1850
13.	MILLARD FILLMORE	1850–1853
14.	FRANKLIN PIERCE	1853–1857
15.	JAMES BUCHANAN	1857–1861
16.	ABRAHAM LINCOLN	1861–1865
17.	ANDREW JOHNSON	1865–1869
18.	ULYSSES S. GRANT	1869–1877

19. RUTHERFORD B. HAYES   1877–1881
20. JAMES A. GARFIELD   1881–1881
21. CHESTER A. ARTHUR   1881–1885
22. GROVER CLEVELAND   1885–1889
23. BENJAMIN HARRISON   1889–1893
24. GROVER CLEVELAND   1893–1897
25. WILLIAM MCKINLEY   1897–1901
26. THEODORE ROOSEVELT   1901–1909
27. WILLIAM HOWARD TAFT   1909–1913
28. WOODROW WILSON   1913–1921
29. WARREN G. HARDING   1921–1923
30. CALVIN COOLIDGE   1923–1929
31. HERBERT HOOVER   1929–1933
32. FRANKLIN D. ROOSEVELT   1933–1945
33. HARRY S. TRUMAN   1945–1953
34. DWIGHT D. EISENHOWER   1953–1961
35. JOHN F. KENNEDY   1961–1963
36. LYNDON B. JOHNSON   1963–

Index